"PIA"
BUSINESS-LIFE ENRICHMENT"
by
KEVIN J. BARKER

"PIA" Business-Life Enrichment program empowers businesses and their employees to achieve excellence in sales and customer service. It also supports individuals in reaching their personal life goals, regardless of their circumstances driving both business success and personal growth.. enables any business and each individual within the business to be at its best in Sales and Customer, Service; enables individuals fulfill life goals, irrespective of the situation or circumstance, enhancing the business bottom-line results and personal growth.

All rights reserved. No part of this publication may be reproduced, stored in a retrieval system, or transmitted in any form or by any means, electronic, mechanical, recording or otherwise, without the prior written permission of the author.

Copyright © 2024 by Kevin Barker
All Rights Reserved
ISBN 9798301136290
Revision of PIA Business Enrichment

DISCLAIMER

This book outlines the author's personal experiences and ideas aimed at improving business performance in Sales and Customer Service, as well as promoting personal growth. The content is provided on an "as is" basis, with no warranties or representations of any kind, including guarantees of increased profit margins, market share growth, or personal development outcomes. The advice and suggestions offered are meant as guides and should not replace your current business plans or personal strategies. Any decisions made based on this book should be carefully considered against your unique circumstances. Use of this book implies acceptance of this disclaimer.

PREFACE

PIA is a trifold enrichment process designed by the author, Kevin Barker, to be applicable in various situations, ranging from overcoming addiction to career advancement, family relationships, financial management, and self-esteem improvement. This methodology centers on establishing purpose, creating an image aligned with that purpose, and cultivating the attitude needed to achieve it.

Drawing on over 20 years of management experience, military service, and coaching, the author combines professional and personal lessons to help readers ascend to greater success in Sales and Service. The book challenges readers to embrace responsibility for their current circumstances and to maximize the present moment while letting go of past experiences. It is written with a sincere desire to help readers press forward toward their goals and embrace positive change.

TABLE OF CONTENTS

CHAPTER 1- What is PIA?   5

CHAPTER 2- Who are YOU?   12

CHAPTER 3- Profitable Customer Service   19

CHAPTER 4- Get the Sales Results You Deserve   29

CHAPTER 5- Completing the PIA Enrichment Process   62

CHAPTER 6- Mental Health   70

CHAPTER 7- Parenting   77

CHAPTER 8- Drug Addiction   89

CHAPTER 9- Marital Discord   94

CHAPTER 10- Career Selection   103

CHAPTER 11- Weight Loss   107

CHAPTER 12- Couple Disputes   111

CHAPTER 13- Quitting Smoking   116

CHAPTER 1 – WHAT IS PIA?

The PIA Enrichment Process—Purpose, Image, Attitude; Passion, Independence, Activity; Patience, Innovation, Accountability—transcends its role as a framework for business or personal growth. It becomes a way of life, a universal tool for achieving greatness in any area, whether improving sales, enhancing customer service, or overcoming personal struggles like addiction. By planting the seed of purpose, cultivating the right image, and sustaining progress with unwavering passion, independence, and action, the possibilities are limitless. The PIA process reminds us that growth, whether in business or personal endeavors, requires dedication, adaptability, and a willingness to hold ourselves accountable. As we nurture our goals with patience and innovation, we discover that success is not just about achieving results but about becoming the best version of ourselves. And just like a flourishing tree, deeply rooted and reaching for the sky, the PIA process ensures that if you grow, everything around you grows as wel

Purpose of This Book

This book is designed to guide you through the process of applying PIA to elevate your Sales and Customer Service performance. To maximize its benefits, approach this material with humility, a genuine desire for improvement, and the commitment to implement PIA throughout your business operations.

The Holistic Approach of PIA

PIA is not just a theoretical framework. While rooted in established business administration principles, its unique strength lies in connecting these concepts to real-world applications. This holistic approach ensures a meaningful, tangible impact on your goals.

Tactical and Strategic Goals in PIA

Tactical Goals

Tactical goals are short-term objectives requiring frequent evaluations—daily or weekly. They involve defined steps that contribute to an overarching strategy.

Strategic Goals

Strategic goals are comprehensive, long-term objectives forming the foundation of your business values. These are evaluated over larger timeframes, such as months or years, and require sustained effort and dedication.

Nature as a Metaphor: Planting the Seeds for Growth

Tactical Goals: Represented by Plants

A tactical goal is like planting a seed that grows into a plant. It requires care, such as watering and sunlight, and periodic nurturing to thrive. Over time, this plant may need to be moved to a larger container to accommodate its growth.

Strategic Goals: Represented by Trees

A strategic goal is akin to planting a tree. Trees develop deep roots, grow tall and strong, and provide shade and shelter for others. Like trees, strategic goals take time to flourish but create a solid, enduring foundation.

Through these metaphors, PIA emphasizes the importance of patience, care, and adaptation in achieving success.

The Three Pillars of PIA: Purpose, Image, and Attitude

1. Purpose

Purpose is the "why" behind your efforts. Clearly defining your purpose is essential for success. For instance, your purpose might be to increase sales revenue, improve team performance, or enhance customer satisfaction.

2. Image

Your business's image should align with its purpose. It reflects how your organization is perceived by customers, employees, and the community. A mismatch between purpose and image can hinder your success.

Example:

If your stated purpose is to provide the best customer experience, yet your business is understaffed and customers face long wait times, the image you project will contradict your purpose.

3. Attitude

Attitude is the glue that holds purpose and image together. A positive attitude, demonstrated by all associates, ensures alignment between these elements. Negative attitudes, however, can undermine even the most well-defined purpose and image.

Addressing Negativity and Uncertainty

The Cost of Negativity

Negative attitudes within a business can spread to customers and the marketplace, damaging your reputation and hindering growth. Unified positivity among employees and leadership is essential for achieving PIA's potential.

The Cost of Uncertainty

Uncertainty in purpose, image, or attitude creates confusion and inefficiency. For example, businesses that fail to communicate their objectives clearly often suffer from disorganized operations and dissatisfied employees.

Implementing PIA in Your Business

1. Identify Your Purpose: Define specific, actionable objectives for Sales or Customer Service.

2. Align Your Image: Ensure your business image supports and reflects your stated purpose.

3. Foster a Positive Attitude: Cultivate an attitude of commitment and enthusiasm among all associates.

Lessons from Experience: Real-World Applications of PIA

Example 1: A Misaligned Image

A linen rental company struggled due to internal conflicts and negative attitudes among departments. By addressing these issues and aligning their purpose, image, and attitude, the company captured a greater market share.

Example 2: The Cost of Poor Training

A logistics company failed to implement PIA principles, resulting in high turnover, inefficiency, and lost revenue. Clear communication and alignment with PIA could have transformed their operations.

Final Thoughts

PIA (Purpose-Image-Attitude) is more than a business strategy; it's a framework for holistic growth. By aligning purpose, image, and attitude across all levels of your organization, you can achieve unprecedented success in Sales and Customer Service.

Your associates must believe in your commitment to them and the PIA process. Without their buy-in, the full benefits of PIA cannot be realized. Use the principles in this book to unify your team and achieve results beyond your imagination.

CHAPTER 2

WHO ARE YOU!

EVERYONE IN YOUR BUSINESS MUST KNOW WHO HE OR SHE IS

Understanding Primary Personality Types for Effective Business Communication

Each person operates primarily from a distinct personality type, occasionally shifting to alternate traits depending on the situation. Recognizing and adapting to these traits within your team and with customers is critical for achieving the best outcomes. Here, we outline four key personality types—Arrow Line, Star, Triangle, and Circle—and offer insights on working effectively with each.

Universal Truths of Business Interactions

- People prefer doing business with those they like.

- Miscommunication often leads to conflict.

- Recognizing and respecting personality differences improves communication and reduces misunderstandings.

By identifying your own primary personality and understanding those of others, you can foster a more productive and harmonious environment for your business.

The Four Personality Types

1. Arrow Line Personality (ALP)

- Key Traits: Self-confident, competitive, persuasive, bold, and results-oriented.

- Strengths: Thrives under pressure and in leadership roles; focused on achieving goals.

- Challenges: Can exhibit excessive competition, leading to conflicts; less tolerant of stagnation and ambiguity.

Tips for Working with ALP:

- Communicate directly and focus on the "big picture" as well as specific details (e.g., Why, When, How, What).

- Avoid small talk; ALPs value logic and results over emotions.

- Be prepared to answer detailed "Why" questions confidently and with evidence.

Customer Example: Customers with ALP traits may push customer service teams to their limits with demanding questions. Maintain composure, remain factual, and clearly articulate how your offering benefits them.

2. Star Personality

- Key Traits: Imaginative, social, ambitious, and open to change.

- Strengths: Thrives in collaborative environments; fosters innovation and builds relationships.

- Challenges: May procrastinate or avoid conflict; tends to focus on gaining approval and exploring numerous options.

Tips for Working with Stars:

- Encourage creative discussions but steer them toward actionable decisions.

- Be firm and straightforward when identifying their critical needs.

- Avoid being overly forceful; instead, guide them toward making decisions confidently.

Customer Example: Star personalities often request multiple proposals to explore all possibilities. Ensure your presentation highlights key options without overwhelming them, and remain patient.

3. Triangle Personality

- Key Traits: Analytical, methodical, practical, and perfectionist.

- Strengths: Excels in structured environments; values logic, order, and standards.

- Challenges: Can be overly critical or controlling; prefers working independently.

Tips for Working with Triangles:

- Provide detailed, logical information to support decisions.

- Respect their time and ensure appointments are well-prepared.

- Offer clear, strengths-focused options without excessive commentary on weaknesses.

Customer Example: Triangle personalities demand data-driven presentations. Highlight how your product or service surpasses competitors, and respect their preference for thorough analysis.

4. Circle Personality

- Key Traits: Trusting, supportive, flexible, and empathetic.

- Strengths: Excels at helping others and values recognition; fosters communication and understanding.

- Challenges: Dislikes conflict and may procrastinate to avoid negative outcomes.

Tips for Working with Circles:

- Actively seek their input to make them feel valued.

- Ask open-ended questions to uncover their needs and preferences.

- Be patient and encourage them to share concerns without fear of disappointment.

Customer Example: Circle customers may avoid voicing dissatisfaction directly. Promptly ask if their needs are met and gently guide them toward a decision.

Applying Personality Insights to Your Business

While individuals can adapt to different personality roles as needed, their primary personality traits will eventually dominate. Rapidly identifying and respecting these traits in customers and associates can:

- Build trust more quickly.

- Reduce conflict and misunderstandings.

- Enhance team collaboration and idea generation.

Encourage your team to recognize and embrace each other's unique strengths, and watch your business thrive with improved communication and mutual respect.

Chapter 3

Profitable Customer Service

Increase the Value of Your Customer's Experience with You

Defining Proactive Customer Service

Proactive customer service means ensuring customer expectations are met before they express dissatisfaction. This approach not only builds loyalty but also protects and enhances profitability.

However, proactive service often requires resources, and management may hesitate to allocate funds. Yet, the costs of reactive service—or poor service—are far greater, leading to lost revenue, damaged reputation, and negative customer perceptions.

Applying PIA (Purpose, Image, and Attitude):

1. Purpose: Ensure every team member is equipped to proactively meet customer needs and resolve issues promptly.

2. Image: Build a brand identity focused on customer care and responsiveness.

3. Attitude: Foster empathy, positivity, and a solutions-oriented mindset across all customer-facing roles.

Proactive Service: A Profitable Investment

When your business commits to proactive customer service, it sets the stage for profitability and growth. Social media magnifies the impact of customer experiences, both positive and negative. Happy customers promote your brand, while unhappy customers can harm your reputation significantly.

Example:

A customer returns a $400 lawnmower. Instead of simply refunding the purchase, apply PIA:

- Purpose: Equip your team to turn the return into an opportunity by identifying the customer's needs and recommending a better-suited product.

- Image: Demonstrate care by addressing the perceived inconvenience and offering a discount or upgraded product.

- Attitude: Approach the situation with empathy, turning a negative experience into a positive one.

This approach not only retains the customer but often results in an up-sell, strengthening long-term loyalty and profitability.

Assessing the Costs and Benefits of Proactive Service

Key Questions to Consider:

1. What is the cost of implementing proactive service?

    - Training employees.

    - Offering small discounts or service solutions.

    - Investing in incentives for customer-facing teams.

2. What is the potential loss of revenue from poor service?

- Dissatisfied customers sharing negative experiences.

- Loss of repeat business and referrals.

- Damage to your brand image.

Applying PIA to Service Costs:

- Purpose: Treat proactive service as a long-term investment in customer retention.

- Image: Highlight exceptional service as a key differentiator in your market.

- Attitude: Commit to a customer-first mindset, valuing satisfaction over short-term savings.

Customer Outcomes and PIA in Action

Each customer interaction results in one of three outcomes:

1. Promoter: Advocates for your brand, encourages referrals, and returns for future purchases.

2. Neutral: May not actively promote or criticize your business, leaving future purchases uncertain.

3. Destroyer: Actively shares negative experiences, discouraging others from doing business with you.

PIA-Driven Approach to Customer Outcomes:

- Purpose: Identify where customers fall on this spectrum after every interaction.

- Image: Use targeted follow-ups and feedback collection to reinforce positive experiences and address concerns.

- Attitude: Train employees to ask questions like, "How can we ensure you would recommend us to others?" This fosters trust and resolution while building rapport.

Building a PIA-Driven Customer Service Team

Proactive, profitable customer service requires a team aligned with the principles of Purpose, Image, and Attitude.

Key Training Areas:

1. Purpose: Equip employees to:

- Build rapport.

- Identify and resolve customer pain points.

- Offer tailored solutions and up-sell opportunities.

- Request referrals from satisfied customers.

2. Image: Ensure your team:

- Reflects the brand's commitment to customer care.

- Handles challenging situations with professionalism and empathy.

3. Attitude: Encourage:

- Positivity and empathy to address customer concerns.

- Ownership of problems to create lasting resolutions.

Selecting the Right Team:

Customer service representatives should display a high level of empathy and lower competitiveness than sales team members. Their focus should remain on customer satisfaction rather than aggressive selling tactics.

Incentivizing PIA in Customer Service

Most businesses reward sales teams with commissions because they generate revenue. However, customer service teams—who retain and grow existing customer relationships—deserve equal recognition.

Example:

A customer spends $5,000 monthly with your company. If poor service leads to their departure in June, the resulting loss until October is $15,000. A $250 incentive to retain that customer through proactive service is a small price to pay compared to the losses incurred.

PIA-Driven Incentives:

- Purpose: Set clear, measurable goals for customer satisfaction and retention.

- Image: Celebrate the role of customer service in protecting and enhancing brand reputation.

- Attitude: Create team rewards that recognize positive interactions, such as bonuses, group outings, or recognition programs.

Budgeting for PIA-Driven Customer Service

To implement PIA effectively, allocate a dedicated customer service budget. This allows your team to address customer needs proactively and strengthens their commitment to resolving issues.

Key PIA Principles for Budgeting:

- Purpose: Treat customer service payouts as essential investments, not optional expenses.

- Image: Transparently share financial performance with your team to motivate and empower better decision-making.

- Attitude: Foster accountability by involving employees in budgeting decisions and results tracking.

Optimizing the Product Return Cycle with PIA

Returned products often represent lost revenue, but a clear return process can turn losses into gains.

PIA-Driven Steps for Returns:

- Purpose: Train employees to handle returns efficiently and identify resale opportunities.

- Image: Develop a return policy that reflects professionalism and customer care.

- Attitude: Encourage team members to treat returns as opportunities to exceed customer expectations.

PIA: A Path to Profitable Service

By integrating Purpose, Image, and Attitude into your customer service strategy, you create a foundation for lasting success. This approach ensures:

1. Customer satisfaction becomes a central goal.

2. Employees feel empowered and motivated to provide exceptional service.

3. Your business enjoys improved profitability and a stronger market reputation.

Final Reflection:

Think about your own experiences with poor customer service. What could have changed your perception? By applying PIA, you can ensure every customer interaction ends positively, fostering loyalty and advocacy for your brand.

Remember: A happy customer is a profitable customer. Invest in your team, implement PIA, and watch your business thrive.

Chapter 4

Get The Sales Results You Deserve!!

(How much sales revenue did you leave on the table?)

To implement the Purpose-Image-Attitude (PIA) framework effectively, the following approach should be incorporated into your sales strategy. This ensures every interaction is purposeful, projects a positive image, and maintains a winning attitude.

Purpose: Clear Goals in Every Interaction

Define the reason behind every sales activity. Each step, whether prospecting, presenting, or following up, should contribute to achieving specific, measurable objectives.

1. Pre-Interaction Planning

- Set clear goals for each customer interaction.

Example: "Identify the top three needs of the customer during this meeting."

- Outline desired outcomes for every call or meeting.

Example: "Schedule a follow-up presentation to propose a tailored solution."

2. Align Efforts with Objectives

- Prospecting: Target customers who align with your company's strengths and products.

- Presentations: Focus on solutions that address the customer's critical needs.

- Follow-Up: Aim to build long-term relationships and generate referrals.

Key Takeaway: Always have a purpose for your actions, ensuring they align with your overall sales goals.

Image: Professionalism at Every Step

Your image represents your company and determines how prospects perceive your credibility and reliability. Leave nothing to chance when shaping your professional image.

1. Appearance

- Dress appropriately for your industry and audience. First impressions matter.

- Maintain a clean, organized workspace during virtual meetings.

2. Communication

- Speak clearly and confidently, focusing on customer value.

- Use strategic answers to elevate discussions, showcasing your professionalism and thoughtfulness.

Example: Instead of simply saying, "We can deliver Monday through Friday," frame it strategically:

"Our delivery schedule aligns with your receiving team's productivity needs, minimizing costs. What day and time optimize your operations?"

3. Brand Representation

• Ensure all materials (business cards, proposals, emails) reflect your brand's professionalism.

• Position yourself as a knowledgeable, solution-oriented expert in your field.

Key Takeaway: A positive image inspires trust and encourages prospects to see you as a reliable partner.

Attitude: Passion Drives Results

Your attitude directly influences your success. A positive, enthusiastic approach attracts customers and creates opportunities, even in challenging situations.

1. Internal Motivation

• Connect emotionally with your product or service. Passion and genuine belief in what you offer create authenticity that customers can feel.

• Stay focused on solutions, not obstacles, during sales interactions.

Example: If a customer rejects your proposal, view it as a learning opportunity to refine your approach.

2.   Customer Interaction

- Project optimism in all communication. Enthusiasm is contagious.

Example: "I'm confident this solution will exceed your expectations. Let's explore how we can make it work for you."

- Stay composed under pressure. If objections arise, listen actively and respond constructively.

3.   Resilience in Prospecting

- Treat every rejection as a step closer to success.

Example: "This 'no' brings me closer to the next 'yes'—time to refine my pitch for the next opportunity."

Key Takeaway: Your attitude fuels your actions and impacts customer perceptions, ultimately determining the results you achieve.

Integrating PIA in Practice

Here's how PIA can be implemented throughout the sales process:

Prospecting

- Purpose: Identify potential customers and schedule meaningful interactions.

- Image: Approach prospects professionally, whether via phone, email, or face-to-face.

- Attitude: Stay motivated, even if faced with initial rejection.

Presentation

- Purpose: Address the customer's critical needs and demonstrate how your solution meets them.

- Image: Deliver a polished, well-prepared presentation that reflects expertise.

- **Attitude:** Maintain enthusiasm for your product, conveying confidence in its value.

Follow-Up

- **Purpose:** Ensure customer satisfaction and foster long-term relationships.

- **Image:** Be consistent and reliable in all post-sale communications.

- **Attitude:** Celebrate successes but always seek feedback to improve.

PIA in Action: A Practical Example

Scenario: A customer inquires about your delivery options.

- **Purpose:** Understand the customer's delivery challenges and present a value-driven solution.

- **Image:** Respond with a strategic answer that positions your company as a partner invested in their success.

Example: "Our flexible delivery schedule is designed to align with your team's needs, reducing operational costs. When would you prefer delivery?"

- Attitude: Present options with confidence and excitement about the value your service will bring.

Summary:

Implementing the PIA framework ensures every sales activity is intentional, professional, and driven by passion. By integrating Purpose, Image, and Attitude into every interaction, you'll not only enhance your sales performance but also build stronger, lasting relationships with customers.

Simply stated, all sales—irrespective of how strong or weak they are—are EARNED. Therefore, don't pass the blame, responsibility, or accountability for your sales results to someone else!! Now that this is understood, then Let's Get the Results That You Really Deserve!!!

Who Is Your Customer?

We will look at this from two separate perspectives:

`1ˢᵗ What demographic group or market segment makes up your current customers.

2ⁿᵈ What demographic group or market segment are you seeking to grow.

Wherever you have a general interest in acquiring new Sales you should focus your marketing, product development, and sales force prospecting activity. Understand you can't totally ignore the other potential Customers. Because if you ignore these markets, your Competition will swoop right in and capture this market share. Therefore, you must maintain a balanced sales plan which encompasses the protection and growth of current markets along with the growth and capture of new markets.

In planning – I am sorry!! Did I say PLANNING? Yes, I did!! In *planning* your prospecting activities, divide out your prospecting time according to your business interest. In other words, you should not focus your time and energy solely on the new market you are trying to capture.

Example:

    Health Care   10%

    Education 20%

    Hospitality 20%

Industrial 5%

Research and Development 5%

Sports/Entertainment 10%

Agriculture 10%

General 20%

*I challenge you right now to access your documented sales prospecting plan. Then go ask your sales representative for his or her documented sales prospecting plan.

Many businesses fail to properly communicate to the sales team the importance of prospecting, particularly the need to minimize any negative interaction with a prospective customer. Because, often it's during the prospecting phase that most prospective customers will have his or her first interaction with the business, often its s/he first level of awareness of your business's existence. Unfortunately, during the prospecting phase often is the only time a prospects has any interaction with a business. Because the experience was so negative it fatally foreclosed any opportunity of future business dealings. Thus, a PIA application focusing on your business prospecting is a strategic target. The Purpose-Image-

Attitude of the prospecting seed needs to be clearly communicated to all associates partaking in prospecting activity.

Furthermore, you are accountable for identifying the target market. This means identifying a target market of customers that will have a specific need for your product and services *and* this market should provide you the opportunity to create a competitive advantage (You Can Actually Provide Something Better Than Their Alternatives) NOTICE THAT I DIDN'T SAY CHEAPER: I SAID BETTER!!

Example: You are an Insurance Salesperson. You need to identify which line of insurance is critical and needed most by an individual or business. Become an expert in this line of insurance. Additionally, you will need to know the strength/weakness of all the alternatives available to your potential customers.

*Just like with the 1st Prospective- you cannot totally ignore the other products within your insurance portfolio. In planning – I am sorry!! Yes, I Did I say PLANNING again! In planning your prospecting activities divide out your time according to how you prioritize the critical essence of the specific insurance product line that you are trying to market.

Example:

    Business Property Insurance- 30%

Residential Property Insurance- 30%

Life Insurance- 20%

Automobile-20%

When you have a genuine interest in the business which you are calling, you will have greater internal motivation in developing your selling skills and enhancing your knowledge. Ultimately, **YOUR POSITIVE ATTITUDE IS GOING TO CREATE YOUR PASSION.**

Summation: *To get the sales results you deserve; you must have a sincere interest in or emotional connection to your TARGET CUSTOMERS and to your PRODUCTS or SERVICES.* In the same way that most people can identify the smell of a skunk, when customers detect your lack of interest or emotion, they will smell that you don't have the passion for what you are presenting and simply won't buy from you. If they eventually decide to buy from you, it will be at a much lower price than what you were expecting and will result in lower commissions/revenue.

Make Contact with Your Customer

Sounds simple? The craziest part is that it really is simple to contact your customer. We (SALESPEOPLE) make contacting the customer more difficult than it should be!!! How do we make it difficult? We find all sorts of reasons to delay the start of our day. Then by the time we do arrive at the customer, the person we seek is either busy or has left for the day. Sound familiar? Unfortunately, Salespeople working in retail stores and other business delay interacting with customers who walk into their business. How many times have you walked inside a business, needing assistance and the staff simply doesn't approach you to ask if you need assistance?

Furthermore, we often determine that the customer won't buy from us before ever making contact. Even worse, we won't call on a customer because the customer previously rejected our sales proposal. I can provide you a whole list of reasons why we formulate the negative mindset that this customer won't buy from us before that initial contact is ever made.

Perhaps the worst of all is that we have an excuse every time we are late to an appointment or, in some cases, simply just don't show up. How many times do we have multiple appointments scheduled for the day? If you are like me, you *want* to have multiple appointments scheduled. Unfortunately, in our quest to have a big day we overbook ourselves and, as a result, don't effectively manage the time at our scheduled appointments. This results to our being late to appointments or missing the appointment all together. When you are late or miss an appointment, the customer really doesn't want to hear your excuse because he has set valuable time aside to meet with you. Appointment scheduling and time management at appointments is critical to business success.

Sometimes we get that one gigantic fish (Prospect) in our sight and simply forget about all the other medium and small fishes that provide us our greatest opportunity. I don't know what your fishing experience is, but there can be a common misperception within the fishing community: the activity is entered with the preconceived notion that a big trophy bass will be caught and mounted on the wall. As a result, needless amounts of money are spent on bait and equipment to catch this elusive fish. In hopes of reeling in the big target, people pass over gear and bait that would easily catch blue gill and other smaller fish. Year in and year out, people depart the lake without the trophy bass and, sadly, often with no fish at all.

Unfortunately, at the end of the day, week or month, our sales results resemble those fish adventures because we have spent all our resources, time and energy chasing that big customer. In the process, we fail to nurture and develop our relationships with the medium and small prospective customers that are readily available to us. Thus, our competition fills their bottom-line profit with revenue from these medium and small prospective customers. Inevitably, those skilled anglers fill their bottom-line profit with big prospects as well by capturing a greater share of the marketplace. By focusing on the one trophy fish, we are conceding the rest of the lake to the competition. It's important to remember that even when we do manage to catch the big customer, the profit from this type of target doesn't equal the profit margins that we enjoy from medium and smaller customers. My point to you is that *you must have a balanced prospecting plan of all prospective customers within your market.*

You must stop finding excuses and go contact your customer!!! Identify who makes the decision along with all the individuals that have an influence in the decision. You find out who the decision makers are by cold calling (Face), cold calling (Phone), Customer Need Surveys, networking and through emailing.

Though before you start working out in the field prospecting you must first create a prospecting plan! Yes, again I refer to the word PLANNING. Your target customer's availability, geographic location, and your specific work environment (Inside or Outside) along with your specific skill set will determine the best approach. Remember that you will need to evaluate all or most of these variables to maximize successful prospecting so allot the proper amount of time.

Example:

* Phone Cold Call of 30%: expect an efficiency rate of 6 to 8%

* Face Cold Call of 40%: expect an efficiency rate of 10 to 12%

* Networking 15%: expect an efficiency rate of 20 to 25%

* Emailing 10%: expect an efficiency rate of 12 to 15%

* Mailing Customer Need Surveys 5%: expect an efficiency rate of 1 to 2%

Why the *expected* efficiency rate? This tells you how much activity you need to get the desired result!

Example:

* Make 40 Cold Calls (FACE) efficiency rate 11% = 4.4 actual results

* Make 60 Cold Calls (PHONE) efficiency rate 7% = 4.2 actual results

FATAL ERROR- At first glance it appears cold calling (FACE) provides the best results–that is until you pose this question: How much time is needed for you to make 40 Face to Face cold calls versus simply picking up a phone and dialing 60 numbers? Don't forget to factor in the cost of fuel—an increasingly volatile commodity! Now make your decision which way is best for you!!

Ok you are out in the field prospecting how do you get to the decision maker that is often protected by lower level of influencers or gatekeepers? First, ask questions that only the decision maker has the answer to or possesses the most validated knowledge. Second, respond to customer questions with a strategic (Big Picture) answer so that when your reply is communicated to the decision maker, your answer reflects a level of value or importance to company authorities. Example: A customer asks about delivery options. **Tactical Answer**: *We can deliver any day Monday through Friday between 8am and 5pm.* **Strategic Answer**: *We partner with you to ensure our delivery time provides you an opportunity to capitalize on your receiving department's staffing and productivity, thus providing you a reduction in receiving costs. We can arrange delivery to suit your needs, Monday through Friday between 8am and 5pm. Which day and time works best providing the greatest positive effect on your receiving costs?* If it's not already obvious, the strategic answer provided your customer with the semblance of carefully acquired options.

Build Rapport with the Customer!

Pay Attention!! This is a critical step to getting the results you deserve. This is not the step to overlook or place minimal effort. Prior to meeting with the customer, you need to gather intelligence about that person. If you cannot find out any information about a specific individual, you should learn something about the company or the neighborhood. In other words, find something!! Utilize the company's Website or Google Search.

Let me share with you this personal experience. I had a large customer that had switched General Managers multiple times in a noticeably abbreviated time period. Each new GM came in with a different vision of which products he wanted featured by the business. As a result, I would have to purchase new product to meet the changing customer's needs. Unfortunately, purchases of the new product were being made prior to our even breaking even on the previous product line. In truth, it was costing us more money to offer business to this customer than the revenue we had gained— even though the customer was a high profile business.

My service representative notified me that another new General Manager had been hired and wanted to meet with me. I scheduled a meeting with the new General Manager and when I arrived in his office, he introduced himself and a woman who was already inside the office upon my arrival. As I sit down, he tells me the history of my company, our performance in the marketplace along with a variety of other details which clearly indicated that he had done his research. He then tells me that he is not only the new General Manager, but he is also the new owner of this business. He also informs me that the woman in the office is his wife and that she would be overseeing the aspect of the business that utilizes my product and services.

The most important question was posed next—one for which I was unprepared: he asks me to share any information I have about his company. My failure to answer his question in detail allowed him to gain the upper hand in the negotiations. He knew I was not going to be aware that he was the owner because he had presented himself to my service representative as just being the General Manager. Additionally, his own staff also thought he was just another new General Manager. Despite his clear dominance of the situation, the good news is that he wasn't interested in making any major changes to the current product, but his wife was interested in expanding the product line which meant greater sales opportunities for me. Although luck was on my side in that instance, I learned never to enter a meeting where the customer arrived with greater knowledge than I had.

*Summation: You should have an approach plan in place that is designed to effectively build rapport. You cannot prepare for every situation, but gathering knowledge allows you to be in a better position to focus your conversation on what really matters.

*Ask the questions and let the customer talk. I don't have to tell you this, but I will: *Salespeople talk too much!!* Your goal is not to persuade the customer so let him dominate the discussion.

Example: You remark about the nice boat parked in the business lot. The customer thanks you for the compliment, and adds, "I take the family out every chance I get." You respond by saying, "My family enjoys boating as well." You have broken the ice, but you need to take advantage of the opportunity to hand the discussion over to the customer by following with, "What is your favorite lake for boating?" Measure the customer's response by making further inquiries or steering the conversation back to the topic. Respect the fact that time is important to people but making them feel valued is equally important.

*It's critical that you use this process to determine the customer's expectation (purpose) during the time spent with you. This can be achieved through your observations or by questioning the customer directly.

Example: "Joe, what is your expectation from our time spent together today?"

*Let the customer know how much time you need with them. Then ask if the requested amount of time works within their plans for that day.

*Do you remember who you are? You identified your dominating personality trait in Chapter 2. Remember that every customer has his or her own unique personality; your job is to identify the personality of the individuals that you are meeting as quickly as possible—ideally within the first 1-3 minutes of meeting them. Why? Because once you identify their dominant trait you will know how to communicate most effectively with them. Assessing that personality type allows you to make your adjustments immediately. Make sure that you keep in mind that a customer's personality trait should dictate the flow of your communication:

<u>Arrow Line</u>- prefers minimum small talk, wants to get down to business and wants to feel like they are in charge.

<u>Triangle</u>- minimal small talk, wants the details, facts, information, and justification.

<u>Circle</u>- enjoys small talk. Be careful because they often have a tough time making decisions. They want to be liked.

<u>Star</u>- Enjoys small talk but prefers to be the center of attention. Let them know how great they will look or how much attention they will receive from the purchase of your product or service.

 Remember in all cases, briefly introduce your company and the benefits that the customer will enjoy from the purchase of your product or services. Example: My company takes pride in its customer service performance. I am supported by a team that clearly understands the importance of exceeding your expectations. We have assisted over 5 thousand businesses like yours to improve their bottom line and we achieve this by providing products that our customers find user-friendly, efficient, and effective in enhancing their business performance.

* Use transitional questions to bridge over into the customer needs assessment.

Example: Mrs. Smith, for me to position my best solution to assist you with improving your business objectives, I need to ask you a few questions so that I get a clearer understanding of your specific needs. What are you looking to enhance by changing from your current supplier? *Listen: they will now tell you exactly what you need to do for them to make a purchase from you.*

*Key Have the customer add your phone number to their cell phone.

Example: Before We move forward, I need you to input my phone number in your cell phone. This way when you need to contact me you don't have to search for my business card.

(Your true benefit is that when the customer is away from the office your phone number is always present and it's easy to refer you to their friends and associates)

Identify Your Customer's Needs!

Let me start off by saying "YES you need a Plan." *Your plan for identifying your customers' needs must be specific and have a downward flow.* You need to uncover the key factors that the customer believes are most important to them. If I stick with my Super Bowl analogy, go big yardage questions early.

Example: What are the top three factors that will drive your decision in selecting your new supplier? What effect do these factors have currently on your business and are they positive or negative?

If the solution to their need is a strength of yours, say "Without a doubt, I can exceed your expectation!

Though before you start providing solutions, you need to explore the customer's other alternatives in meeting the needs that you have identified as being critical. It's very important to have a clear understanding of your strength and weakness in comparison to your competitor's strength and weakness. This is simply another necessary part of planning and preparation: know the solution alternatives before walking into that meeting. You will achieve this after having performed the following:

1- Identified the customer's top three factors they consider in making a purchasing decision.

2- Positioned your strength to meet their needs. *If you don't have a strength to meet their needs, be honest and direct with the customer by saying something along the lines of, "I have a solution to your needs but it might not be the best option available for you in the market place."*

I am sure some of you just shook your head in disbelief as I made that recommendation to you, but I want you to look at the big picture: if the customer *does* make the decision to purchase from a different source, it happens with a full understanding of your product weakness and strength. This is yet another way to empower the customer because you will have provided all the information needed to make an intelligent buying decision. Additionally, most customers will appreciate your honesty. Honesty is the foundation for LONG-TERM SELLING RELATIONSHIPS.

By completing that carefully executed pass in the previous steps, you are able to provide your customer with the best solution or product to meet each specific need. When communicating your solution, it's very important that you break your presentation into three separate distinct categories:

1-Present the features of your product and services. Key- Remember that unless your company has the patent rights to the product, features can be matched by your competitors.

2-Present the benefits the customer will experience from selecting your product or service and how this isn't available to them from any of the other alternatives.

3-Stress the value of the product or service and how it will affect the customer. Key- Establishing those solid relationships will remind the customer that he enjoys doing business with you instead of someone else. Additionally, I noticed that most salespeople are excellent in presenting the features of their product. Where most salespeople fail is by not effectively presenting the advantage, benefit, and value to the customer. The majority of salespeople tend to "feature dump" and hope that they say something that catches the customer's attention.

Why is that most salespeople are afraid to present the price? Could the following be the reasons why?

   1-They do not have a clear understanding of the customer's alternative options.

   2-The salesperson knows s/he has dropped the ball in presenting value.

   3-The Salesperson lacks the emotional connection/or passion for the products-services that they are selling.

   4-They don't know the type of buying situation they are

encountering.

Most customers fall into one of these three types of buying positions:

1-Commodity – Customer is simply interested in the lowest price. They have little or zero concern regarding quality, service, or product performance. (Represents 20% of buying decisions)

2-Prime- Customer wants a good product/or service at a fair price. These customers often disguise themselves as commodity buyers. Remove their disguise by presenting your commodity (low end) product/or services. If they reject for any reason other than price, they just told you that they are not a commodity buyer. If they still don't buy, they simply did not see the value in what you are offering for the price you are seeking. (Represents 70% of buying decisions. The questions you ask and the responses you provide will move their value perception of your product or services up or down)

3-Peak- Customer who wants the best product or service and is willing to pay the price. They have low tolerance for their expectations not to be met. They expect excellence from all levels- you, product, services, and support process. If you offer a price that is too low or discounted, you will lose the customer because you will devalue your offer below their expectations.

Example:

If we are shopping and see something at a price of 5 to 15% off the regular ticket cost, we think that's a good deal. If we see something 20 - 30% off, we think this must be clearance. When we see something discounted 30% and greater we start looking for defects. Do not devalue yourself, product, or services by offering discounts without justifiable reason. You must state your price with confidence! Remember if you are successful in uncovering the customer's critical needs and presenting the advantages and benefits effectively, the customer perceives value. Ultimately, the customer will have already made the decision to buy from you, prior to you presenting your price.

Ask for the Customer's Buying Commitment (Close)!! *OOPS!! The fact is that way too many times the close opportunity is missed because the salesperson is not listening or simply fails to ask the customer for a buying commitment. You must ask the customer for their business.

(GET THE SIGNATURE)

Example: When do you want your first shipment? I need you to sign right here!!

If you present your total package and the customer only raises price as a concern, s/he has basically communicated to you that s/he is happy with the product and service that you have offered and is ready to buy from you! Take a breath and start the negotiation process. The customer is simply questioning the value of your offer or doesn't have the financial resources for the particular price. So how do we address this small speed bump?

To begin with, you should have already prepared a negotiating strategy plan prior to going to your appointment. You must always take into consideration the buying situation that you are facing. *You must effectively communicate the customer's cost incurred by NOT buying from you.* You need to know what you are willing to give up and what you need from the customer for you to lower your price.

Example: Larger Order, Guaranteed long term purchase agreement:

1-At what point do you stop negotiating? What amount is too unreasonable?

2-Never walk away from the table! Some salespeople will say, "Let me make a phone call while you take time to think" or offer a variety of other reasons not to close the deal at that moment. This is a sign to the customer that he has the upper hand.

*Key never break the silence—verbally or non-verbally. The first to speak loses!!

Upon coming to an agreement, immediately ask for the customer's signature. Unfortunately, most salespeople start telling the customer how happy they will be with the product and that a good decision was made. This needless chatter opens a whole new line of possible questions/or objections from the customer.

Simply stated: shut up and get the signature. After you get the customer signature and complete all applicable paperwork. Then, ask the customer this question, "What could I have done differently to make our meeting more efficient and productive? The customer's answer will provide you ammunition to enhance your next presentation to a customer.

WOW! We get the contract or purchase order and disappear! Why? You should always follow up with your customers. When you fail to follow-up with your customer, you are showing that you didn't have confidence in your solution or that the product meeting your customer's need. That's why you are afraid of what concerns or complaints await you if you make a follow-up call.

You should follow up immediately upon customer receipt of your product or services. Ask the customer the dreaded question, "Did our product or services meet your expectations? What can we do for you to improve your level of satisfaction? If the customer communicates that s/he is happy, immediately ask s/he for any referrals s/he may have for you. Get the email and stay in contact while sharing the various promotions you may have, news relating to the customer that you come across and on all holidays. Make sure you keep your name in front of the customer. Don't rely on a business card. Have the customer input your phone number in his or her cell phone. Remember this should have been done during your introduction to the customer.

But I don't want to forget one of the most common excuses for not securing the customer's business "OUR PRICES ARE TOO HIGH; THEY WONT EVER BUY AT OUR PRICE." This is a rationale that sounds all too familiar. The truth that we need to recognize is that price was not the issue! We failed to effectively present our product or services. The result? The customer doesn't recognize the value needed for them to sign the purchase agreement. Because we have failed to uncover the customer's key needs, the customer does not see the benefit of buying with us. We often fail to identify these "Key Needs" because of our poor questioning or listening skills. The point I am making to you is that if we don't properly identify our key customer needs and effectively present a product or service that is going to meet or exceed these key needs, it's virtually impossible for the customer to perceive the value in what we are offering at a high enough level to buy from us. We sometimes allow ourselves to be misled by those customers who do buy from us because we believe we have done an excellent job as salespeople. In most cases, the customer just did not have any viable alternatives to us. Your attitude and your passion is the driving force to your Sales results!!

Sales is a number game as well. You need to know what you need to do to earn the income you desire.

Example: You want to make $80,000.00.

-Commission Rate 8%

-Average Sale $5K

-Prospecting Efficiency 9%

-Close Rate 20%

Commission Rate:

Therefore, to enjoy a $80,000 income, with a 8% commission rate. You will need to generate $1million dollars in sales ($1mil sales*8%=$80k income)

Average Sale:

The average $amount of your sales per customer will determine the total number of customers that you need to sell for you to generate the $1million in sales.

Example: If your average sale is $5k. You will need to generate 200 sales ($1mil/$5k= 200 sales)

Prospecting Efficiency:

Additionally, your expected prospecting efficiency is going to determine your total number of prospecting activities to generate the desired number of sales appointments.

Example: If your prospecting efficiency is .09%, to have

1000 sales appointments. You will need to have 11,111 prospecting activities (1000/.09=11,111 activities)

Close Rate:

Additionally, your expected close rate is going to determine the number of proposals that need to be presented to customers.

Example: If your closing rate is 20%, for you to have 200 sales. You will need to present 1000 proposals (1000*20% close=200 sales)

Number of Field Days:

Furthermore, you will need to factor in how many days you will be available to work in the field. I am going to utilize 230 field days. Why not

365 days? I subtracted out days for holidays, vacations, sick days, meetings and based it on a 5-day work week. Now that you know the number of days that you expect to be working in the field 230. You can now determine your daily activity.

Example:

Prospecting 11111 year/230= 48.3 activities a day

Sales Presentations 1000 year/230= 4.3 appointments a day.

The majority of people have a buying process. If you don't have a sales plan you are at the mercy of the customer!! Always show up for your appointment. Call the customer in advance if you are going to be late. Make a friend, find a way to win, even when it appears you are in a no-win situation. If the customer is a no show, call on neighboring business or residents.

Additionally, identify what is really important to the customer. Their answer will tell you exactly what you need to provide to earn their business. Always speak with confidence when you communicate your price.

Chapter 5

Completing the PIA Business Enrichment Process

In Chapter 1, I introduced the concept of PIA—Purpose, Image, and Attitude—as the foundation of the enrichment process and the first step to aligning your actions with your goals. At that level, we explored identifying your PURPOSE, embodying your IMAGE, and cultivating the right ATTITUDE, likening it to planting a seed to grow in harmony with the universe.

Now, let's delve into the second and third levels of the PIA enrichment process, which build upon this foundation to create a comprehensive path toward fulfillment and success.

2nd Level of PIA: Passion, Independence, and Activity

Passion

Passion is the fuel that powers the fulfillment of your PURPOSE. Without it, neither you nor your team can sustain the energy necessary to navigate challenges. Passion acts as the unwavering force that propels you forward, even when obstacles arise.

Think of a time you ran out of gas in your car before reaching the station. The frustration, unpreparedness, and the detour that followed all stemmed from not maintaining the energy source you needed. In business, a lack of passion can similarly cause your progress to sputter to a halt. Even the most well-laid plans and intentions can falter without the vitality that passion brings.

Passion ensures that you and your associates remain motivated and resilient, refusing to give up on the PURPOSE you've set out to achieve. It energizes every action and shields your efforts from discouragement.

Independence

Independence ensures that your focus remains firmly fixed on your own PURPOSE, free from the distractions of external goals or influences. This autonomy is vital for achieving clarity and commitment to your objectives.

Imagine tuning a radio. When the signal isn't clear, competing songs and static distort the intended message. Independence is like adjusting the tuner until your station comes through, undisturbed and crystal clear. Similarly, by fostering independence, you eliminate distractions and dedicate your resources—time, energy, and focus—toward the PURPOSE that matters most.

A lack of independence can lead to hesitation, indecision, or reliance on others for validation. Independence, however, empowers you to act decisively and prioritize your PURPOSE over external expectations or competing interests.

Being "in-between"—neither fully committed to your goals nor fully detached from competing priorities—creates stagnation. True independence demands unwavering dedication to nurturing the seed you planted in the first level of the PIA process. Without it, your progress will stall.

Activity

Activity is the visible manifestation of your commitment to your PURPOSE. It measures the alignment between your efforts and your goals. But not all activity is effective; purposeful actions, taken at the right time and with the right resources, are essential.

For example, cold-calling prospective clients is a measurable activity. If you make 20 calls in a day and secure three appointments, your effectiveness is 15%. To improve results, you have two options:

1. Increase activity: Make more calls to achieve more appointments while maintaining the same success rate.

2. Improve effectiveness: Secure more appointments from the same or fewer calls by refining your approach.

This principle applies universally: whether you aim to enhance customer service, sales, or operational efficiency, purposeful activity reflects your priorities and provides benchmarks for improvement.

Activity must also align with both PURPOSE and IDENTITY. It's easy to claim focus and discipline, but your actual actions reveal where your time and energy are truly directed. Through consistent, effective activity, you unlock the full benefits of the PIA enrichment process.

3rd Level of PIA: Patience, Innovation, and Accountability

Patience

Patience is indispensable when pursuing long-term objectives. Delays, setbacks, and unforeseen challenges are inevitable, but patience allows you to maintain focus and positive energy despite them. Without patience, frustration and negativity can permeate the team, hindering progress and collaboration.

Consider a scenario where your team adopts a new customer service software to improve satisfaction ratings. Initial usage rates may be low due to inadequate training or resistance to change. Patience, coupled with effective communication, enables you to guide your team to success instead of reacting with frustration or blame.

Patience is about creating an environment where growth can occur naturally, even in the face of challenges. It fosters resilience, encouraging you and your associates to persist until the desired outcome is achieved.

Innovation

Innovation is the ability to adapt and find creative solutions to unforeseen challenges. As you journey through the PIA process, unexpected hurdles—financial constraints, regulatory changes, or market shifts—will test your resolve. Innovation empowers you to overcome these challenges by thinking outside the box and reimagining traditional methods.

To innovate effectively, you must be willing to challenge norms and embrace change, even when it feels uncomfortable. Remember, your PURPOSE is unique to your business, and fulfilling it requires adaptability and a willingness to explore new approaches. By prioritizing innovation, you future-proof your efforts and maintain momentum, regardless of external disruptions.

Accountability

Accountability ensures that the responsibility for fulfilling your PURPOSE lies squarely with you. Success or failure in the PIA enrichment process is a direct result of your actions—or lack thereof.

Reflect on the foundational elements of the PIA process. Did you clearly define your PURPOSE? Did you and your team embody the IMAGE required to support it? Was your ATTITUDE aligned with your goals? Did you sustain the PASSION to persist, the INDEPENDENCE to prioritize, and the ACTIVITY to make progress? Were you PATIENT and INNOVATIVE when challenges arose?

By holding yourself and your team accountable, you eliminate excuses and maintain focus on the ultimate objective. Accountability demands reflection, adaptability, and a commitment to continuous improvement. It reinforces the principle that each day is a new opportunity to advance toward your PURPOSE, unburdened by past failures.

PIA: A Living Process

The PIA enrichment process is a dynamic and ongoing journey. Just as a plant or tree requires consistent care to grow, so does your PURPOSE. By cultivating Purpose, Image, Attitude; Passion, Independence, Activity; and Patience, Innovation, Accountability, you create a sustainable framework for success.

"If your plant and tree grow, you grow as well."

CHAPTER 6- MENTAL HEALTH

The PIA Enrichment Process is a structured, nature-inspired framework designed to help individuals identify and achieve personal growth by aligning their Purpose, Image, and Attitude with actionable steps and universal principles. Its unique focus on connecting personal development to the growth of plants or trees serves as a grounding and transformative metaphor for life. Here's how it can assist someone battling fear, anxiety, depression, or low self-esteem:

Who Am I?

I am your guide to applying the PIA process to your personal challenges, offering clarity, actionable insights, and encouragement. My purpose is to support you in connecting with your inner strength and resilience, using PIA as a roadmap for overcoming obstacles and enriching your life.

How Can PIA Assist You?

Purpose: Who Are You and What Do You Want to Achieve?

• Self-Discovery: Help you uncover your deeper aspirations, whether it's overcoming anxiety, rediscovering confidence, or breaking free from depression.

• Clarity: Define clear, achievable goals that give you direction. For example:

• Short-term purpose: "I want to reduce anxiety by practicing mindfulness for 10 minutes daily."

• Long-term purpose: "I want to feel confident enough to speak in group settings."

Image: How Do You See Yourself?

• Positive Self-Perception: Assist you in creating a positive mental image of yourself. For example, if you struggle with low self-esteem, we would focus on qualities you admire and want to embody.

- Alignment with Purpose: Ensure that your thoughts, actions, and self-image reflect the person you aim to become.

Attitude: The Glue That Holds It Together

- Mindset Shift: Teach you how to adopt a growth mindset that embraces challenges and setbacks as opportunities.

- Consistency: Cultivate attitudes that reinforce your purpose and self-image, ensuring your inner narrative aligns with your external actions.

Second Level: Implementation for Emotional Well-Being

Passion: Reignite Your Inner Flame

- What excites you? Identify activities, people, or ideas that spark joy or curiosity. For instance, reconnecting with a forgotten hobby can build momentum for emotional healing.

- Fuel for Challenges: Use passion as the energy source to move through tough times, reminding yourself why growth matters.

Independence: Focus on Your Journey

- Detach from External Noise: Guide you in setting boundaries and tuning out comparisons or judgments from others, so you can fully focus on your goals.

- Reclaim Ownership: Empower you to prioritize your well-being above all else, reinforcing your ability to achieve emotional independence.

Activity: Small Steps, Big Results

- Plan and Act: Break your goals into manageable tasks. For example:

  - If battling fear, create a plan to face it gradually (e.g., start with controlled exposure to a feared situation).

  - If struggling with depression, schedule small daily activities that bring satisfaction, like journaling or a short walk.

- Measure Progress: Track your actions and reflect on how they bring you closer to your purpose.

Third Level: Sustainability and Growth

Patience: Trust the Process

• Accept Setbacks: Help you develop patience by reminding you that growth, like a tree, takes time. Mistakes and slow progress are part of the journey.

• Stay Calm: Foster a calming perspective to navigate delays or obstacles without self-criticism.

Innovation: Try New Approaches

• Think Outside the Box: Explore creative ways to address challenges, like experimenting with different therapeutic methods or self-help practices (e.g., art therapy, group support, or meditation apps).

• Adaptability: Guide you to pivot when traditional methods don't work, maintaining momentum.

Accountability: Own Your Growth

- Reflect and Adjust: Encourage regular self-assessment to ensure your actions align with your purpose. Celebrate small wins to build confidence and resilience.

- Ownership: Remind you that your growth is your responsibility, empowering you to stay committed.

An Example of PIA in Action: Overcoming Fear of Social Interaction

1. Purpose: "I want to feel comfortable introducing myself to new people at events."

2. Image: Visualize yourself as approachable and engaging.

3. Attitude: Replace self-doubt with curiosity about others' experiences.

4. Passion: Focus on how building connections enriches your life.

5. Independence: Avoid comparing yourself to extroverts—embrace your unique style.

6. Activity: Start by attending small gatherings and speaking to one new person.

7. Patience: Accept that progress might be slow but steady.

8. Innovation: Use social skills workshops or practice conversation starters.

9. Accountability: Reflect on each interaction and adjust your approach.

By planting the metaphorical seed of growth and nurturing it through the PIA framework, you can reconnect with your inner strength, overcome emotional hurdles, and thrive. "If your plant and tree grow, you grow as well."

CHAPTER 7- PARENTING

Using the PIA Enrichment Process to Assist Parents with Disrespectful, Unruly, or Unmotivated Children

Step 1: Purpose

- Define the Parent's Purpose: The parent's goal might be to foster a respectful and motivated child. This should be specific and measurable, such as "encourage better behavior and communication within the next three months."

- Define the Child's Purpose: Help the child identify a purpose, such as excelling in a hobby, school, or building better relationships at home.

Step 2: Image

- Parent's Image: The parent should reflect the image they wish to instill, such as being patient, fair, and firm. This means modeling respectful behavior, even in stressful situations.

- Child's Image: Discuss the image the child wants to project (e.g., "Do you want to be seen as a kind, capable, and motivated person?"). Help them visualize the benefits of embodying that image.

Step 3: Attitude

- Parent's Attitude: The parent's attitude must align with their purpose and image, showing consistency in responses and a willingness to listen while setting boundaries.

- Child's Attitude: Teach the child how their attitude affects their ability to achieve goals and how a shift in attitude (towards positivity or perseverance) can make their purpose attainable.

Step 4: Enrichment Activities (2nd Level of PIA)

1. Passion:

- Help the child discover passions (e.g., sports, arts, or academics). Use these as motivational tools to encourage better behavior.

2. Independence:

- Gradually allow the child to make choices and take responsibility for their actions, fostering autonomy and accountability.

3. Activity:

- Plan structured, positive activities. For instance, set tasks like creating a daily routine, helping with household chores, or participating in extracurricular activities.

Step 5: Reflection and Accountability (3rd Level of PIA)

1. Patience:

- Recognize that change takes time. Celebrate small victories and remain calm in setbacks.

2. Innovation:

- Use creative approaches to address problems. If traditional discipline isn't working, try positive reinforcement, collaborative problem-solving, or new communication techniques.

3. Accountability:

- Both parent and child must be accountable for their roles. The parent commits to consistent rules, and the child is encouraged to accept consequences for their behavior.

Practical Example: Homework Resistance

1. Scenario: A child refuses to do their homework and talks back when asked.

2. Application:

- Purpose: Improve the child's sense of responsibility toward schoolwork.

- Image: Model calm, consistent communication. Explain how being diligent with homework reflects on their character.

- Attitude: Encourage positive reinforcement like, "You worked hard today; I'm proud of your effort," and stay firm but kind during conflicts.

- Passion: Connect homework to their interests (e.g., "If you love video games, math can help you understand game design!").

- Activity: Set specific, achievable goals for homework completion and celebrate progress.

- Accountability: Discuss consequences for not doing homework and stick to them (e.g., limited screen time).

Incorporating "Who Are You" Framework

Step 1: Identify Personalities

- Parent's Personality: The parent reflects on their primary personality type (Arrow Line, Star, Triangle, Circle). For example:

    - Arrow Line (ALP): Assertive and goal-oriented.

- Star: Social and imaginative.

- Triangle: Analytical and detail-oriented.

- Circle: Supportive and relationship-focused.

- Child's Personality: Identify the child's dominant personality through observation and discussion. For example:

- A child who resists strict rules but thrives in creative tasks might have a Star personality.

- A child who prefers clear instructions and predictability might have a Triangle personality.

Step 2: Adjust Parenting Style Based on Personality

1. Arrow Line Parent with Star Child:

- Conflict Potential: The parent may focus on results while the child wants freedom and creativity, leading to clashes over rigid expectations.

- Adjustment:

- Allow the child some flexibility in how tasks are completed.

- Emphasize the connection between creativity and achieving goals.

2. Circle Parent with Triangle Child:

- Conflict Potential: The parent may prioritize emotional support, while the child wants structure and detailed plans.

- Adjustment:

- Provide clear, step-by-step instructions while offering encouragement.

- Show how the child's logical strengths can help others.

3. Star Parent with Arrow Line Child:

- Conflict Potential: The parent may focus on collaboration, while the child prefers to take charge and make decisions independently.

- Adjustment:

- Give the child leadership opportunities in appropriate areas.

- Use positive reinforcement when they show cooperation.

Step 3: Strengthen Communication

1. Match the Child's Communication Style:

- Arrow Line Child: Be direct and focus on the "big picture."

- Star Child: Engage in brainstorming and praise their creativity.

- Triangle Child: Offer detailed explanations and logical reasoning.

- Circle Child: Emphasize trust, patience, and emotional connection.

2. Build Trust:

- Let the child know their personality is understood and valued. For example, tell a Circle child, "I really appreciate how you always think about others."

Step 4: Resolve Conflicts

1. Use Personality-Based Techniques:

- Arrow Line Child: Avoid emotional arguments; focus on facts and logical consequences.

- Star Child: Reduce tension by using humor or creativity to address the issue.

- Triangle Child: Provide structured solutions and clear reasoning behind decisions.

- Circle Child: Address conflicts with empathy and reassurance.

2. Collaborative Problem-Solving:

- Example: If a Triangle child resists cleaning their room because the task feels overwhelming, the parent can break it down into steps and work alongside the child to demonstrate support.

Step 5: Foster Motivation

1. Leverage Strengths:

- Arrow Line: Set measurable goals and let them track progress.

- Star: Create opportunities for creative expression in tasks.

- Triangle: Provide logical rewards for completing tasks.

- Circle: Offer praise and emphasize the positive impact on others.

2. Involve the Child:

- Engage them in planning tasks or setting family goals based on their personality type. For instance, a Star child might enjoy designing a reward chart, while a Circle child could thrive by leading a family meeting to resolve conflicts.

Example in Action: Homework Resistance

Scenario: A Circle parent with a Triangle child struggles to get the child to complete homework on time.

- Step 1: Recognize the child's need for structure and logic.

- Step 2: Provide a clear plan with milestones (e.g., "Complete math problems 1-5 by 4 PM").

- Step 3: Use the parent's supportive personality to praise efforts: "I love how focused you are on making sure your work is correct."

- Step 4: Reflect together on what worked and adjust the plan if needed.

By using the PIA Enrichment Process and the "Who Are You" framework, parents can create a structured, understanding, and growth-oriented environment tailored to their and their child's unique personalities and needs.

You can now copy and paste this entire document.

CHAPTER 8- DRUG ADDICTION

To use the PIA (Purpose, Image, Attitude) enrichment framework to assist someone battling drug addiction, you can adapt the principles described in the document to focus on personal growth, resilience, and goal-setting in recovery. Here's an example:

Applying PIA to Support Recovery from Drug Addiction

1. Purpose

- Define the Purpose: Begin by identifying the person's core motivation to recover. This could include reconnecting with loved ones, improving health, regaining independence, or achieving personal goals.

- Exercise: Encourage the individual to write down their purpose and visualize it daily. For example, they might plant a small seed (literally or metaphorically) to symbolize their commitment to growth and change.

2. Image

- Create a Positive Self-Image: Help the individual envision the person they want to become in recovery. Discuss what it means to be healthy, confident, and fulfilled.

- Exercise: Have them develop a list of affirmations or a vision board that reflects their desired self-image. This image should align with their purpose.

3. Attitude

- Foster a Positive Mindset: Cultivate an attitude of hope, determination, and openness to change. Explain that setbacks are part of the journey and can be learning opportunities.

- Exercise: Suggest daily reflection or journaling to monitor their attitude and make adjustments when negative thoughts arise.

4. Passion

- Reignite Interests and Passions: Help the person find activities or hobbies that spark joy and serve as positive outlets.

- Exercise: Encourage them to dedicate time each week to an activity they love, whether it's art, music, exercise, or volunteering.

5. Independence

- Encourage Self-Reliance: Support the individual in setting boundaries and avoiding situations or relationships that may trigger relapse.

- Exercise: Work on developing independence through setting small, achievable goals (e.g., attending therapy sessions, managing finances).

6. Activity

- Stay Active in Recovery: Consistent, positive actions reinforce purpose and growth. This includes attending support meetings, engaging in healthy habits, and participating in therapy.

- Exercise: Track daily activities and reflect on how each contributes to the recovery journey.

7. Patience

- Practice Patience in Progress: Recovery is not linear. Emphasize the importance of patience with oneself and others.

- Exercise: Use mindfulness techniques to stay calm and present during challenging times.

8. Innovation

- Adapt to Challenges: Encourage creative problem-solving to overcome obstacles in recovery.

- Exercise: Brainstorm new ways to handle triggers or stress, such as trying new relaxation techniques or joining support groups.

9. Accountability

- Take Responsibility: Foster a sense of ownership over their recovery process.

- Exercise: Pair the individual with a mentor or accountability partner who can provide support and hold them to their commitments.

By using the PIA framework, recovery becomes a structured and meaningful process that emphasizes personal growth, resilience, and connection to a larger purpose.

CHAPTER 9- MARITAL DISCORD

Using PIA and Personality Insights to Support a Married Couple Battling Marital Issues

I. Applying the PIA Framework

The PIA (Purpose-Image-Attitude) enrichment process can assist a married couple by guiding them to reflect on and improve their relationship through structured self-awareness and actions.

1. First Level: Purpose-Image-Attitude

- Purpose:

  - The couple identifies shared goals, such as fostering a loving, respectful, and supportive partnership.

  - Example: Building trust and enhancing communication as a team.

- Image:

- Reflect on how they want their relationship to be perceived, both publicly and privately.

- Example: They may wish to be seen as a unified, supportive couple by friends and family.

- Attitude:

- Commit to attitudes of kindness, patience, and mutual respect to align their purpose and image.

- Example: Both partners work on demonstrating empathy and understanding during disagreements.

2. Second Level: Passion-Independence-Activity

- Passion:

- Reconnect with the passion that brought them together, such as shared hobbies, date nights, or reminiscing about their early relationship.

- Independence:

- Each partner maintains a sense of self while respecting their individual needs and boundaries.

- Example: Both partners agree to personal growth through individual hobbies or therapy.

- Activity:

- Actively engage in behaviors that strengthen the relationship, such as attending counseling sessions, practicing conflict resolution, or creating time for one another.

- Example: Weekly check-ins to discuss emotions, needs, and progress in the relationship.

3. Third Level: Patience-Innovation-Accountability

- Patience:

- Practice patience during setbacks, recognizing that lasting change takes time.

- Example: One partner may struggle to improve communication, but patience ensures progress is supported, not rushed.

- Innovation:

- Adopt creative approaches to resolve recurring issues or introduce new bonding activities.

- Example: Learning communication techniques like active listening or nonviolent communication.

- Accountability:

- Each partner takes responsibility for their actions and commits to improving areas of personal weakness.

- Example: Acknowledging and addressing mistakes instead of shifting blame.

Practical Metaphor: Planting and Growing

The couple could plant a tree together as a symbolic act of nurturing their relationship. As they care for the tree, they remind themselves that their relationship also requires consistent care, effort, and attention to thrive.

II. Incorporating the "Who Are You" Framework

Understanding personality types (Arrow Line, Star, Triangle, and Circle) can further strengthen the couple's relationship by improving communication, reducing conflicts, and fostering mutual appreciation.

1. Identify and Understand Each Other's Personality Traits

Each partner can explore their own and their spouse's primary personality traits. For example:

- Partner A might identify as a Triangle Personality (analytical, methodical, practical).

- Partner B might identify as a Circle Personality (supportive, empathetic, flexible).

2. Enhance Communication and Conflict Resolution

- Tailor communication to align with personality traits:

- A Triangle Personality prefers logical and detailed explanations.

- A Circle Personality values empathy, understanding, and emotional connection.

3. Foster Appreciation for Differences

- Instead of viewing personality differences as sources of conflict, appreciate them as complementary strengths:

- The Triangle Personality brings structure and organization.

- The Circle Personality strengthens the emotional bond and promotes harmony.

4. Navigate Stressful Situations

- Recognize exaggerated traits during stress:

- A Star Personality may procrastinate.

- An Arrow Line Personality may become overly assertive.

- Adjust responses to de-escalate conflicts and promote understanding.

5. Build a Stronger Team Dynamic

- Recognize that each partner contributes unique strengths to the relationship:

- For example, an Arrow Line Personality may lead decisively, while a Star Personality contributes creativity and innovation.

6. Use Open-Ended Questions to Connect

- Use open-ended questions to uncover each other's needs and perspectives:

- Instead of assuming why the Triangle Personality is upset, ask, "What's the biggest concern you have about this situation?"

- Instead of criticizing the Circle Personality for being indecisive, ask, "How can I help you feel more comfortable making this decision?"

III. Practical Application Plan

1. Self-Assessment: Each partner reflects on their own and their spouse's primary and secondary personality traits.

2. Personality Discussions: Share insights about personality traits and how they influence behavior, communication, and decision-making.

3. Conflict Analysis: Analyze past conflicts to identify how personality traits influenced actions and reactions. Develop strategies to handle similar situations in the future.

4. Personal Growth Plans: Each partner sets goals for improving interactions, such as practicing patience, empathy, or clearer communication.

Conclusion

By combining the PIA framework with insights from the "Who Are You" personality content, couples can build a deeper understanding of themselves and their relationship. This approach fosters empathy, improves communication, and strengthens their ability to work together as a cohesive and resilient team, ultimately enriching their partnership and paving the way for a healthier, more fulfilling relationship.

You can copy this formatted document into any text editor or word processor for further use. Let me know if you need any additional edits or customization.

CHAPTER 10- CAREER SELECTION

The PIA (Purpose, Image, Attitude) framework can help someone identify the best career path by fostering personal and professional enrichment through self-awareness and goal alignment. Here's an example application:

Step 1: Purpose

Action: Reflect deeply on what drives you and what outcomes you want in life and work.

- Example: If your purpose is to positively impact the environment, this could steer you towards careers in sustainability, renewable energy, or environmental science.

How PIA Helps: By identifying your core purpose, you can focus your efforts on career paths that align with your intrinsic motivations.

Step 2: Image

Action: Consider how you want to be perceived by others, such as peers, employers, or the community.

- Example: If you aim to project an image of innovation and leadership, careers in technology, entrepreneurship, or research may fit.

How PIA Helps: Ensures that your career aligns with your desired personal and professional brand.

Step 3: Attitude

Action: Assess your mindset and approach to achieving your goals.

- Example: If you thrive on collaboration and mentorship, fields like teaching, counseling, or team management may be ideal.

How PIA Helps: Reinforces the importance of maintaining a positive attitude to bridge your purpose and image effectively.

Application of Second and Third Levels

- Passion: Identify fields that excite and energize you.

- Independence: Seek careers where you can focus on your goals without distractions.

- Activity: Take practical steps like internships, informational interviews, or volunteering to gain experience.

At the third level, you'll need:

- Patience: Be prepared for challenges and gradual progress.

- Innovation: Find creative ways to navigate obstacles or pivot within your career.

- Accountability: Take full responsibility for your career growth by setting measurable milestones.

Example Outcome

Let's say an individual identifies their purpose as helping others, their desired image as a trusted advisor, and their attitude as empathetic and collaborative. Based on these, they might pursue a career in social work, counseling, or human resources.

Through this process, PIA helps individuals connect their internal motivations with external actions, ensuring their career choice supports long-term fulfillment.

CHAPTER 11- WEIGHT LOSS

The PIA (Purpose, Image, Attitude) framework from your document can support substantial weight loss goals by applying its principles across the three levels of enrichment:

1. Purpose, Image, Attitude (Level 1)

- Purpose: Clearly define the weight loss objective (e.g., "I aim to lose 50 pounds in one year to improve my health and energy levels").

- Image: Visualize how you want to be perceived internally and externally—healthy, disciplined, and confident.

- Attitude: Maintain a positive and determined mindset, ensuring your actions align with the purpose and the image you want to project.

Example Application: Begin by planting a literal seed in soil to represent your commitment to this goal. Nurturing the seed symbolizes the care and consistency needed to nurture yourself during this journey.

2. Passion, Independence, Activity (Level 2)

- Passion: Cultivate excitement about achieving the goal by associating it with activities you love, like cooking nutritious meals or joining a fitness class you enjoy.

- Independence: Focus on your personal journey, avoiding comparisons with others. Customize your strategies (e.g., meal plans or workouts) to fit your unique needs and preferences.

- Activity: Establish measurable activities, like exercising 5 days a week or tracking daily caloric intake, to ensure steady progress.

Example Application: If your goal is to lose 1 pound per week, track activities like meal prep and workouts. Measure outcomes and adjust for improvement, much like tracking cold calls in a business setting.

3. Patience, Innovation, Accountability (Level 3)

- Patience: Understand that weight loss is a gradual process. Remain steadfast through plateaus and setbacks by focusing on long-term progress.

- Innovation: Experiment with new approaches, such as interval training or alternative diets, to keep the process engaging and effective.

- Accountability: Hold yourself responsible for your goals. Use a progress journal or work with a coach to ensure consistency.

Example Application: Create an accountability system by setting up weekly check-ins with a friend or coach. Use setbacks as opportunities to innovate, such as adjusting your routine if a current one isn't yielding results.

Final Note

The PIA enrichment process integrates physical actions (e.g., planting and nurturing a seed) with reflective and actionable goals, providing structure and motivation for a weight loss journey. By following its principles, the journey becomes a holistic growth experience, ensuring sustainable results.

CHAPTER 12- COUPLE DISPUTE

To help a non-married couple overcome relationship issues using the PIA enrichment process, the following approach can be applied:

1. Purpose: Identify shared goals and values.

- The couple should articulate their primary relationship purpose. For example:

    - Strengthening emotional intimacy.

    - Building trust and communication.

    - Planning for long-term commitments like cohabitation or future family goals.

This process allows them to recognize their collective objectives and align their efforts toward mutual benefits.

2. Image: Define the perception of the relationship.

- Reflect on how they see themselves as a couple and how they wish to be perceived by each other and others. For instance:

  - "Do we want to be seen as supportive partners?"

  - "What kind of energy and behavior do we bring into the relationship?"

Ensuring their relationship image aligns with their purpose can eliminate misaligned behaviors or expectations.

3. Attitude: Foster a healthy mindset.

- Both partners need a positive attitude that supports their purpose and image.

- Example: Commit to empathy and open-mindedness during conflicts.

4. Passion: Rediscover mutual interest and connection.

- Rekindle shared passions or explore new hobbies together to reignite energy in the relationship.

- Passion provides the emotional energy needed to address challenges and celebrate growth.

5. Independence: Maintain individuality.

- While focusing on shared goals, each partner should retain a level of independence, pursuing personal growth and interests.

- This ensures balance and prevents enmeshment.

6. Activity: Take action to improve the relationship.

- Purposeful activities such as:

- Scheduling weekly check-ins for honest conversations.

- Setting aside time for dates or shared activities.

- Attending relationship workshops or therapy.

7. Patience: Navigate setbacks calmly.

- Recognize that rebuilding trust or improving communication takes time.

- Avoid reacting harshly to mistakes, and allow each other space to grow.

8. Innovation: Find creative solutions.

- Think outside the box to solve recurring issues. For example:

- If communication is a problem, they could explore structured formats like using a "talking stick" or journaling to express feelings.

9. Accountability: Take responsibility.

- Each partner should hold themselves accountable for their actions and their impact on the relationship.

- Example: Apologize sincerely when at fault and make consistent efforts to improve.

Additional Tools: Personality Dynamics

Using the four personality types (Arrow Line, Star, Triangle, Circle), the couple can identify their primary traits and how they affect their interaction. For instance:

- An Arrow Line partner may prioritize efficiency and directness, while a Circle partner may prefer emotional connection and support.

- Recognizing these differences can lead to tailored communication strategies that respect both personalities.

Symbolic Actions

- Plant a seed together as a metaphor for their commitment to nurture the relationship. The growth of the plant serves as a reminder of their effort and progress.

By applying the PIA enrichment process, the couple can systematically address their challenges and strengthen their bond through self-awareness, shared efforts, and ongoing development.

CHAPTER 13- QUITTING SMOKING

Using the PIA enrichment process can be highly effective in assisting someone trying to quit smoking by structuring their journey into actionable, reflective steps. Here's how it can be applied:

First Level of PIA: Purpose, Image, and Attitude

1. Purpose:

Define a clear purpose, such as "I want to quit smoking to improve my health and be a better role model for my family."

- Planting a small seed can symbolize this goal. Care for the seed daily, as a reminder to care for your well-being.

2. Image:

Create a mental or external image of yourself as a non-smoker.

- For example, visualize how quitting will enhance your image as a healthier, happier person. Share this image with your support system for accountability.

3. Attitude:

Maintain a positive and proactive attitude toward quitting.

- Embrace setbacks as learning opportunities, not failures. Display confidence that you can overcome the addiction.

Second Level of PIA: Passion, Independence, and Activity

1. Passion:

Stay passionate about why you want to quit. Write a list of personal benefits and revisit it when motivation wanes.

- Example: Increased energy, saving money, or being able to climb stairs without getting winded.

2. Independence:

Distance yourself from triggers or environments that encourage smoking.

- Avoid social gatherings where smoking is prevalent or ask friends who smoke to support you by not smoking around you.

3. Activity:

Replace smoking with healthier activities.

- Engage in exercise, meditation, or hobbies like painting or gardening to keep your hands and mind busy.

Third Level of PIA: Patience, Innovation, and Accountability

1. Patience:

Understand that quitting is a journey with ups and downs. Practice patience with yourself.

- Celebrate small milestones, such as one smoke-free day, a week, or a month.

2. Innovation:

Explore new tools and techniques to quit.

- Use apps that track progress, try nicotine replacement therapies, or experiment with mindfulness-based approaches like deep breathing exercises when cravings hit.

3. Accountability:

Hold yourself accountable by tracking progress or involving a trusted friend or mentor.

- Example: Share weekly updates on your progress with a support group or counselor.

Symbolic Connection:

The metaphor of planting and nurturing a seed or tree serves as a daily reminder of your growth. As you water and care for your plant, reflect on the time and effort you're investing in yourself to break free from smoking.

By integrating the PIA process, you build a holistic, mindful approach to quitting smoking, aligning your actions with your goals while staying grounded and motivated.

Made in the USA
Monee, IL
24 December 2024

42ad143f-ac3f-4227-8f32-70aef950ed58R01